Improv(e) Your Conversations:
Think on Your Feet, Witty Banter, and Always Know What To Say with Improv Comedy Techniques

By Patrick King
Dating and Social Skills Coach at
www.PatrickKingConsulting.com

Table of Contents

Introduction

How many people can you name that can do passable, if not flat-out hilarious impersonations of Janet Reno, George W. Bush, Alex Trebek, and Robert Goulet?

There is only one man who possesses the talent to do such a thing: **Will Ferrell**.

For those that are unfamiliar with Will Ferrell, he is a stand-up comedian, actor, and improv comic that was one of the primary drivers of **Saturday Night Live's** revival during the 1990's.

He was also one of the first people that was an "**automatic**" for me.

Anything he released, acted in, or was involved in, I would without question automatically watch it. Whether he was the second coming of laughter itself or his mannerisms just **resonated** with my personal sense of humor, Will Ferrell was one of my early role models and my first "**man-crush**" during my impressionable years.

Somewhere down the line, probably from Wikipedia, I

learned that he essentially got his start in the comedy world through **improv comedy**.

Obviously, if I was going to follow in the steps of my man-crush, I needed to investigate improv comedy as well.

I had somewhat more mixed results than Mr. Ferrell, epitomized by the practice where I misinterpreted someone's scenario as a very personal insult. In less subtle terms, I **sucked**.

I was just unable to follow the very, simple rules of improv comedy because I was too **self-conscious**. It was the classic case of being too in your own head, which fuels the cycle of self-consciousness and **impaired performance**.

I was just too focused on **rehearsing** what I wanted to say in my head, which prevented me from truly listening to others. I would listen to them, but ignore the signals and direction they were giving me and stubbornly proceed on my own path. I **waited for my turn to speak**.

In my head, I thought that I already knew what the **outcome** and trajectory of a scenario would be, so anything that was even slightly dissimilar from that threw me off monumentally. I didn't allow for the possibility of tangential directions, and was not confident enough to simply go with an **unfamiliar flow**.

If you think those are bad in **conversation**, they're exponentially worse in improv comedy, where my partners had to build off the stuttering mess I was giving them.

Thankfully sooner rather than later, one of my friends sat me down and explained that my approach was fundamentally wrong.

Improv is a **group dance** that ebbs and flows with what each member of the group is doing. The group always stays together, because even if you're unfamiliar or uncomfortable with a certain type of dance, you'll be supported and helped by others through it to work towards a **shared goal**.

I eventually improved quite a bit, but my career in improv comedy was doomed to be short-lived and untapped.

About 3 months after I started coaching clients full-time, I realized that perhaps my attempt to be the second Will Ferrell could still pay off in some way. It occurred to me that just about everything I was teaching clients about social interaction, conversation, thinking on their feet, and witty banter – they were all intimately similar to the lessons I learned in improv comedy.

Improv comedy above all else teaches **flow**, and the ability to make **something out of nothing** – both of those things in pursuit of a common shared goal of a lasting interaction and deep connection with the people involved.

Sound familiar to how a great conversation should be?

Often, people feel like they lack flow, embody awkwardness, and simply have nothing to say to other people. They also feel like they want to walk away from a conversation with a better understanding of the other person, with a connection made.

Well, what better way to improv(e) your conversations than to integrate principles integral to improv comedy? These are principles and rules that have been developed over **years** of real practice and study to address the same exact issues and goals that conversations pose.

Eliminate awkward silences and make conversation flow smoothly? Listen better, go deeper, and connect effortlessly? Verbally banter and spar without having to think about what to say? Ditch self-consciousness and put yourself into unfamiliar situations? **Check, check, check**.

Let's take advantage of the **framework** that improv comedy has laid down for us, and discover how and why improv comedy players never run out of things to say, always seem sharp and witty, think quickly on their feet, and give the best witty banter in the world.

Chapter 1: Just improv(e) your conversations!

Great conversations don't just appear spontaneously out of thin air.

You might get lucky once or twice with someone that just happens to be on the same **wavelength** as you, but that's a rare occurrence and it's not going to happen often. How can you emulate that feeling of a great, flowing conversation with **anyone** you meet, **anywhere** you go?

This doesn't happen without preparation and planning.

But planning in this sense isn't rehearsing scripts and trying to think of interview questions to mask awkward silences. If you have a **flowchart** for conversations, you're doing it wrong and are probably digging a deeper hole for yourself.

Here's the planning you need: if you want your conversations and interactions to be more insightful and effective, you need to have a basic understanding of the **anatomy** of a great conversation.

A great conversation greatly resembles **improv comedy**, and should ideally involve almost all of the same basic rules that I'll cover in this book.

If you've ever seen an improv comedy show, you'll know that they call themselves **players**, and treat it like a **sport** rather than a performance. This is significant, because it instantly frames what you see on stage as a **collaborative** process where everyone is helping everyone else. They are constantly working towards a **common goal**, and understand the flexibility and sacrifices required to reach it.

If none of that resembles how you've approached conversations or interactions up to this point in your life, it's time to re-evaluate that approach!

It takes a lot of training, and some improv comedians have spent years **toiling** away to get their craft right – that wit, playful banter, and conversational intelligence doesn't happen overnight.

Spontaneity and flow.

Improv comics take each performance on its own terms, and come in with **zero expectations** about where it should be leading. This mindset by itself is transformative in creating a sense of openness and **flexibility** that gives life to great conversations.

They don't have an agenda, and are completely comfortable with the fact that they will be establishing something new based on playing off each other. Their flow inevitably fits the mood of their audience and other comics.

If you come into a conversation with a certain expectation

about how it will go, or you want to push it into a certain direction, you're going to disrupt any type of flow you establish. Flexibility and the ability to adapt to fit someone's mood are paramount to any great conversation.

It's the difference between reading a script like a **robot** and actually speaking like a thinking human being.

<u>Being emotionally in tune.</u>

What separates great improv from lousy improv is how in tune the comics are with other people's **emotions** that are being conveyed.

Players will often outright state their emotions and how they feel, and it's up to the other players to **react** to that accordingly in ways that advance an interaction. It's simple, but we don't often do this or catch this in daily conversation.

When you understand the emotional state of your audience and other players, you are basically given a **template** for where to go, and when to go there.

It's all about seeing the given **emotional boundaries** for your conversation, and catering towards what people are conveying and want to talk about. Once you're clear about the message and tone that is desired, you can act accordingly. All it takes is a little bit of **observation**, and being willing to deviate from any blueprint you set for an interaction beforehand.

Once you're clear about these boundaries and know what

you can and can't say, it's much easier for you to get people to feel comfortable with you.

The crowd is naturally comfortable around great improv comics because they know they aren't in for any negative surprises – the comic makes the interplay of emotions and feedback smooth and doesn't leave others hanging. Even awkward moments are made **endearing and charming**. A lousy comic totally misreads the crowd and takes them down roads that aren't interesting or pleasant. They come off as standoffish, oblivious, or like they aren't listening.

Think about how this applies to daily conversation. If someone conveys that they are angry or sad and we completely **miss** it, an awkward and uncomfortable situation arises. We think they're being weird and standoffish, while they think we are being oblivious and insensitive.

It's really that simple, but grossly overlooked in practice.

Establishing fun.

Most people like to talk to people that are fun. When you break it down, there are only a few **benefits** that people receive from conversations, and **fun and entertainment** is a major one.

Guess what one of the goals of improv players is? They do it because they love it and have fun with it. They get their willies by making crowds **laugh**. They simply establish a fun **atmosphere** where people enjoy themselves, and you can tell the enjoyment on the players' faces when they are on stage.

If you are able to establish a fun atmosphere in your conversations, people will simply enjoy being around you more and subsequently will open up to you more. The more **likable** someone is, the closer they are to the keys to the kingdom.

It's just **human nature**.

One of the keys to creating fun is to let go of the standard interview questions, **filter you less**, and think outside the box. There is an entire chapter dedicated to this concept later.

There's no right or wrong.

Great comics know that there really is no such thing as a right answer.

All they're shooting for is to establish an atmosphere of **flow**.

If they establish that atmosphere of **collaboration** and working towards a common goal, they know that they will be **supported** in any direction they go. This is extremely comforting, and allows them to take leaps of faith that might be high-risk and high-reward. It allows them to not play it safe, if they know that they will never crash and burn because of the support of their players.

If you want to become a better conversationalist, always understand that you're not engaged in a debate. There is no right or wrong answer. What you're shooting for is to establish an atmosphere of **likeability and collaboration**. You want the person listening to you and talking to you to like you. That is your end goal, and that's difficult when you are constantly debating, arguing, selling them, or trying to change their minds.

They might **not** know it, but you are helping them work towards a common goal of a great interaction. Anything else is just a slight detour that still points to the same goal.

The power of improv.

Improv comedy is one of the best things you can do for your ability to think on your feet, excel at witty banter, and just know what to say. Conversation is a **learned** skill that takes practice, so it's time to realize that and consciously practice it.

Many people stray from social interaction and conversation because it can be so **unpredictable**. *What if it's awkward, they hate you, think you're weird, or don't laugh at any of your jokes?*

This compels some people to essentially have a **script** in their head every time they talk to people, in an attempt to make it more unpredictable and more comfortable. But that's not reality. If you use a template, just one detail that doesn't fit the template can throw the conversation off. You'll be lost even worse than before.

You can't have a script, and there's no step-by-step process that you go through to create great conversations each and every time. We must realize that each and every moment ebbs and flows with an emotional energy, and we must cater to it.

Perhaps improv is better phrased as using a **situation-based** approach to social interaction and conversation. When you know the **emotional and contextual situation** that is being conveyed, you have your guidepost, compass, and map. It's much easier to think on your feet when you have those, isn't' it?

Chapter 2: Always say "Yes, AND..."

Rule of Improv Comedy: In response to someone else's suggestion, thought, or topic, always say "Yes, AND..." to move to their topic and add something to it, to keep the conversation flowing.

If you want your conversations to flow smoothly, you have to seize the **power of possibility**.

You're not looking to **filter** anything from entering a conversation. You're not saying that certain subjects are not allowed, taboo, or unimportant.

Instead, you're constantly saying **Yes!** and allowing topics to go in whatever **direction** they naturally flow. Any direction is possible, and should be unless you're in an interview of some kind.

Adopting the mindset of Yes, AND..." means that you are **collaborating** with the person that you're talking with. It means that you are accepting the things and subjects that they bring to the table and working with them by **adding** to it – this preserves a flow, keeps them interested in the conversation at hand, and makes interactions as smooth as butter.

At its root, this is a chapter about recognizing where people may want to go in a conversation, and meeting them there.

For example, if somebody says something about Middle East policy, instead of showing disinterest and changing the subject because of negative objections you have to that topic, you embody "Yes, AND..." and you talk not only about Middle East policy, but **add** how that affects economic issues in Africa.

Another example: if someone is talking about their favorite kind of pizza, you reply with "Yes, AND the restaurant that serves that kind of pizza the best is right around the corner!"

Another example: if someone states that the air conditioner is on way too strong in the conference room, you reply with "Yes, AND I can't believe that the salespeople are all in short skirts!"

Instead of throwing your conversation partner off and telling that person that you want to talk about something else, you carry that person **deeper** into the conversation by talking about (with the first example) economic consequences in addition to the politics of the topic. Similarly, if somebody is talking about a new scientific discovery, you can discuss the **additional** commercial uses of that scientific discovery.

Instead of walling off a conversation and saying you'd rather talk about something else, you bring in a deeper and more comprehensive level of analysis. This highlights your intelligence, but it also highlights your **emotional engagement**.

You send a signal to the person that you're talking to that what they are saying is important to you... and by bringing in other areas for discussions, you show additional interest in fleshing out the details of that topic. This enables you to push the conversation forward, but also direct it to where you want it to go.

An added bonus is that you make your conversation partner feel extremely **heard and validated**, and that just makes them enjoy talking to you even more.

"Yes, AND..." reinforces emotions.

When you use "Yes, AND..." you **inevitably** end up sending the right emotional signals to the person you're conversing with. Whatever they are conveying, you are **agreeing** with. You become an **ally**. You become somebody that they can trust.

You may not necessarily agree all the time, but the beauty of the phrasing of "Yes, AND..." is that you initially do agree outwardly, even if you follow it up with something that doesn't necessarily support them.

This creates an agreeable context and opens the way for the other party to conclude that you understand how they think. At the very least, you've created an opportunity for a feeling of **mutual understanding**.

For example, when people are angry or upset, they often just want to be heard and have an **outlet** for their rage. "Yes, AND..." automatically gives them one, and you will instantly become "a great listener" and someone that is understanding and sympathetic.

Compare this with "Yes, BUT..."

"Yes, AND..." is a great statement because it carries people in and enables them to converse on a deeper level. It enables you to demonstrate how you think to that other person.

This can lead to all sorts of intimacy. At the very least, it opens an opportunity for the person that you're talking with to feel that you get them.

However, if you use the phrase, "**Yes, BUT...**", you immediately come off as **combative**. You come off as if you're arguing with them or you are trying to correct them. This turns the conversation into a power struggle. Instead of an ally, you come off as an **adversary** obviously trying to take control of the agenda.

Recall that improv is about accomplishing a **shared goal**. This requires flow, working together, and accepting what other people bring to the table regardless of what it is. That's the essence of "Yes, AND..." and the opposite of "Yes, BUT..."

It's really important to understand the differences between these two. You want to come off as somebody that is working with the flow instead of actively trying to debate and cut somebody off.

There are no right or wrong answers, only answers that lead to flow and those that do not.

Your agenda and shared goal is simply to create an **environment** where you can get the other person to trust you and make them feel that you are a friend. "Yes, AND..." makes people feel heard, validated, and that you are willing to go with them wherever they lead.

A great conversation has a million different directions, and you must be open to all of them.

Try this exercise:

Constantly agreeing with someone can be difficult, especially if you don't quite agree and just need to keep the flow of a conversation.

Have a friend come over and begin a conversation with them. You may only answer with "Yes, AND..." to anything they say. When you get used to it, have them talk about issues and things that they know you don't like. This will force you to dig deep, exercise your creative half, and find the positive insight in any topic that arises.

Chapter 3: React every single second.

Rule of Improv Comedy: React to everything put in front of you, because it was probably put there for a reason.

Great improv comedy is never an **intellectual** exercise.

When you tell a story on a purely intellectual level, it can easily become boring and rote. It can easily be perceived as some sort of a lecture.

Effective stories contain moments that beg reactions from the audience. These stories make clear what's **important**, and what you should get worked up about.

It's like a covert invitation that we all follow when we listen to stories, or laugh when a friend tells a bad joke. You just know the reaction they are seeking because you see that they worked for it and dropped hints as to the reaction that they wanted.

By keeping an eye out for **hints** that people leave for the reactions they want, you can increase the likelihood that your conversations will be longer, more emotionally engaging, and lead to where you want them to go.

<u>People drop hints in conversations for a reason.</u>

There's a reason why people you talk to tend to **dwell** on certain things. On some level, those aspects and details of the conversation are important to them, and their dwelling is a hint that they want you to run with it as well.

If you simply talk about those aspects and lead it back to them personally, they will get a huge sense of acknowledgment. They feel that you get them and appreciate them.

In other words, you're setting the stage for them to feel good about you.

This is why highly effective sales people are so effective. They know that, deep down inside, people are very thirsty for acknowledgment and the respect that underlies that acknowledgment. When you are clear as to the hints being dropped by the person talking to you, you only need to explore those sub-topics to get that person to feel that you are acknowledging them. You are obviously talking about something that they care about. The more they feel that they matter, the more they like you.

Unfortunately, people who are looking to become better conversationalists focus primarily on the **subject matter** to establish trust.

That might work in an academic setting, but it doesn't in a casual conversation. So it's really important to let the very deep-seated human need to be respected, acknowledged and appreciated work to your favor and it all boils down to emotional engagement.

Just listen better and try to figure out what's important to the other person. People usually don't outright say that they want to talk about certain topics, so it's up to you to pick up on their hints and react accordingly.

For example, if someone keeps talking about their dog or seems to mention them in an offhand manner some way, this is a breadcrumb for you to follow, Inspector Holmes. Again, rarely will people say "I want to talk about my dog, listen to me now" as opposed to shoehorning it in semi-organically into an existing conversation.

Be affected and show reaction.

When people share certain details with you that you know they want reactions to, it's okay to be a little bit **exaggerated** in your reaction.

You have to remember that there is a thin line between being profoundly emotionally touched by somebody's shared information and **mocking** that person by basically caricaturing their emotions. If you go overboard, you might come off like you're mocking the person and you will alienate them emotionally. They will feel judged, and probably won't open up to you anymore.

This is the complete opposite of the respect and appreciation that they crave.

Show **appropriate** levels of emotional reaction. If you're able to do this properly, this lets them know that you care about what they're talking about. Also, what they are saying is as important to you as it is to them.

For example, this is a gasp, a grand gesture of happiness or anger, a clenching of your fists, or a huge chuckle.

If they come to you with a story about how they were slighted, show **appropriate anger**. You get the idea. It doesn't even have to be a matching emotion, it just has to show reaction and acknowledgment, which is what people are seeking most of the time. The next step is to throw in a "Yes, AND..." to go deeper on their hint.

Again, exaggerate to an extent.

Unfortunately, different people have different **emotional intensity levels** and in many cases, and the middle of the bell curve as far as emotional expressions is concerned can be quite wide.

What I mean by this is you have to be extra dramatic for people to accurately read your emotional reaction. If you were to simply just react like you would normally react, this might still be too subtle for it to be accurately read by the person that you are conversing with.

In this case, a little exaggeration is needed just so you can clearly show your emotional reaction. Again, you are exaggerating to communicate clearly to the person that you're talking to that you get what they are saying and that you are affected.

Some of us have poker faces far more than we realize, so exaggeration is sometimes necessary to get any message across.

<u>React to move in the direction that you want.</u>

If you want to be a really good conversationalist, you have to be **adaptable** and prepared to move in the direction of the person you're talking to.

Conversations are two-way streets and sometimes you have to take a **detour** you don't want.

If you are always hell-bent on moving the direction where you want your conversations will inevitably hit a wall.

But **strategically** using your reactions, you can shift the direction to a middle ground that is more acceptable to both of you, and eventually to a topic that you want.

How do you do this?

For example, if someone comes to you angry, you don't have to show reciprocal anger. If you don't want to talk about their source of anger, just acknowledge it, and display a strong emotion of your own to change gears. The **strength** of the emotion is key, because they can't ignore that. They in turn will react to your emotion, and the conversation will take a totally different direction.

And if someone comes to you to share a video that you couldn't care less about, you laugh and react, and show a strong emotion to pivot the conversation.

Don't feel that you are at the mercy of the person you are talking to as far as conversation topics.

A conversation is a two-way street.

You can't simply just say what you want to say, wait while the other person is talking and then say what you want to say again. It's not just a simple matter of waiting for your turn to speak.

It's about others **sharing** something with you and being simultaneously being **affected** by what you share. You acknowledge the ideas and the information that they're sharing so that they become emotionally engaged.

Acknowledge the importance of what they're saying. This means that what is important to them has an emotional impact on you. Remember, people are always looking to be acknowledged, appreciated and respected.

If you want your conversations to go deeper, last much longer and lead to mutual admiration and mutual familiarity, you need to play this game. Reactions **aren't** natural to all of us, and we may not even care about most of the things that people say. Some of us have **poker faces**.

That's fine, but make an effort and realize that that you're working towards a goal here, and that can require a little bit of sacrifice and work.

You're not going to master it overnight. However, the

sooner you start in emotional exaggeration and sending off the right emotional signals of appreciation, the higher the likelihood that your conversations will lead to where you want them to lead.

<u>Try this exercise:</u>

Tell a friend what you're doing here, because they will be confused at first. You are now silent and on mute. You cannot talk, while a friend that you are having a conversation with can still talk.

It is a completely one-sided conversation, where you must express yourself through your reactions only. Facial expressions, body language, gestures, and eye contact. Exaggerate them and make sure that your true message is getting across. It probably gets across the vast majority of the time!

This is practice for you to react to others, and see what the range of reactions can be to demonstrate that you've heard them. You may also discover that you have to exaggerate your reactions a bit to be understood, and that something that seemed so obvious to you actually was not.

Chapter 4: Use specific statements, not open-ended questions.

Rule of Improv Comedy: Don't force others to answer broad questions because it puts a conversational burden on them and interrupts banter.

We ask questions all the time because they come easily to us.

We often **navigate** the world based on questions, and **wondering** about what we see, hear, and know.

But if you're trying to get a great conversation going, questions, especially **open-ended** ones can lead to **minefields**.

Remember that great conversations involve a **frictionless** back and forth. Topics just come up naturally in the minds of the two people talking, and there is no limit as to what they can and will share. This doesn't happen when you continually ask questions that stop people in their tracks, make them dig deep, and take them out of the present.

Open-ended questions make people work.

When you ask open-ended questions like, "What do you like to do for fun?" this has a tremendous impact on the free flow of the conversation.

The recipient of the question ends up having to do a lot of work. Answering an open-ended question like that takes a lot of **mental work**. The more open-ended the question, the more work is involved. This has a net effect of forcing your conversation partner to stop whatever they're doing just to come up with a reply.

How do you really answer that question of what you do for fun, anyway? *Uh... I like to go running sometimes and watch movies.*

A better example would be "Have you seen any good movies lately" or "Have you seen the latest Toy Story?"

One more: "Are you into working out at all? I love the gym."

Worst of all, when you ask open-ended questions, you put the burden of keeping the conversation going on your partner. The examples above are easily answered, and will lead somewhere.

Instead of feeling that they are equal partners in keeping the conversation going and contributing to a flow of easy information, they feel **overburdened**. They feel that the conversation has become **imbalanced**. In many cases, they feel that they're doing all the work and you're just sitting back there shooting out all these questions. Eventually, it becomes more of a **chore** rather something enjoyable.

Not surprisingly, when people feel that they are being **interrogated**, they start resorting to simple one-sentence answers. The sentences keep getting shorter and shorter until the conversation pretty much freezes. Instead of feeling that you're doing a scene together, asking too many questions shifts the conversation. Eventually this leads to a chill in the air and the conversation stops.

<u>The more specific your questions the better.</u>

If you feel that you can't really continue the conversation without asking questions, you need to ask specific questions.

The reason why open-ended questions poison any kind of conversation is because they put a lot of **interpretive work** on the part of the person who is supposed to answer. They have to filter the question and then make a **judgment call** as to what's the question is really asking. They have to dig for information that would answer the question.

In many cases, they might feel that the question is so broad that whatever answer they come up with would fall short. That's too much responsibility for any one side of a conversation.

This is why it's really important for you to try to ask very, very specific questions. Very specific questions are easier to answer because they often only require **one** piece of information. This is good news because when people are prompted to supply this piece of information, the person asking can then contribute to follow up on that question or with a statement. It's much better than simply asking somebody to explain themselves with a very open-ended question. It simply **maintains flow**.

Another advantage of specific questions is they allow you to **direct** a conversation depending on the specific answers given. This enables you to read the emotional signals you're getting from the person you are talking to and direct the conversation to that direction by asking a specific question that gets you there.

"Do you like to play basketball?" A simple yes or no answer, and you can be on your way with your next topic of conversation. Or you can dig deeper into their answer if you wish to go into that direction. It doesn't pause the conversation, make your conversation partner work too much, and is easy for both of you.

A **more** specific "Did you play basketball in high school" is an even easier question to answer, and preserves flow better thusly.

Leading statements are even better.

Instead of asking questions at all, use leading statements.

When you use a statement, you come off as **giving** information. You come off as **contributing** to the conversation because you are inserting information.

You help **build** the conversation instead of taking from it. That's what happens when you're simply just asking questions - you're requesting information and you're taking it. The great thing about statements is you can still ask questions, but in a friendlier way. When you use statements that include information, your conversation partner has an easier job. They can either confirm or deny it and explain. In other words, instead of putting them on the spot, you can put a statement out there and they can then feel that they can **contribute**.

A specific question might be "Did you like that painting?" This is better than an open-ended "So do you like art?"

A **statement** to similar effect might be "That was an amazing painting." Or "You liked that painting, didn't you."

Another example: "That was a movie with an amazing amount of explosions and nothing else." Instead of "Did you like all the action that was in that movie?"

Another example: "This coffee is stronger than the Incredible Hulk!" instead of "Do you think this coffee is strong?"

Statements serve the same purpose by **forcing** your conversation partner to answer, but they do it in ways that are easier, subtler, and **more conversational** than questions. Using leading statements instead of questions are essential to the flow of a great conversation, and will remove any barriers that your conversation partner will have in getting there. They have the exact same effect as a question, but are easier, smoother, and less interview-y.

It's as simple as this – statements make interaction and

conversation easy for people to engage in because they don't require massive amounts of thinking, and create a great conversational flow.

<u>Try this exercise:</u>

You are not allowed to ask questions. Converse with a friend and seek to use statements like the example above to elicit responses from them.

Say you watch a movie. Talk about how the movie was great and how much you loved the characters. They will respond to the negative or positive, and the conversation will flow from there.

Chapter 5: Be as present and observant as possible.

Rule of Improv Comedy: Be as present and observant as possible so you can see where an interaction is coming from, and where it wants to go.

If you were to analyze really successful improv comedians like Jim Carrey, you will notice that he have a great knack for being **in the moment**.

He's able to do this exactly because he **pays attention** to all the signals his audience is sending out. He knows exactly what they like and don't like, and he is able to craft his response based on the signals he sees.

Without his **observation skills**, he will have no clue whether his jokes, pacing, tone of voice, and even subject matter will hit a funny bone.

Improv comedy is all about being present and observing your audience and conversation partners to figure out exactly what they are giving you, so you can decide where to go.

The good news is that this is not as hard as you think. We

do this all the time already, but we don't do it as **consciously** as we should. I'm talking about a combination of body language, posture, facial expressions, tone of voice and other expressions of their current feelings. We notice when people feel strongly about things, but anyone can **plainly** see those.

You need to keep your eye on the big picture and piece all these different signals together to send out the right signals to the person that you're talking to – the little things are what matter the most.

This is what separates highly effective improv comedians that kill it every time and those who simply fall flat. It's not really a question of who can tell a better **joke**. Success in improv comedy turns more on how well you can read the moment.

If you want to be a very effective conversationalist, you need to also pay attention to the micro signals and hints being sent.

If you can **observe and interpret** expressions of feelings, vocal tones, facial expressions, body language and the overall flow of the conversation, you will connect far better than you ever have. You'd be surprised as to how clear these signals are and how effective they are in giving what you need to know to stir and manage the conversation the right way.

Your new goal should be to emulate **Sherlock Holmes**, and make a judgment call about every little detail you see someone give you.

<u>Learn how to read your conversation partner to direct the conversation.</u>

Many times when conversations die, it's because you have a **fixed** idea of what you wanted to say, and the conversation **deviated** and left you confused and speechless. It's understandable that you want to prepare as much as possible for a conversation, but it's not always ideal.

When you prepare and focus on what you need to say next, you are the opposite of present. You are stuck in your own head, and not listening or observing at all – you're just waiting for your turn to speak. This is a very common **error**. The **results** are also very common.

Nine times out of ten when you do this, the conversation simply fades until it finally dies. You have to remember that regardless of whom you are talking to, they probably don't want to talk to you in a way that follows your **script**. In fact, they probably want to talk about something completely different, and you have to leave yourself open to that.

The first step to this is getting outside of your own head and really listening to how they **react** to your statements. Be present and observe everything about their reactions.

By being a little more **selfless**, your conversations will become a little bit more interesting.

<u>Learn to pick up on small hints.</u>

Whenever you talk to somebody about a particular subject,

they're **always** sending out signals regarding how they feel about what you're talking about.

It takes quite a bit of practice to get a clear and accurate read of these signals. Don't expect an accurate read each and every time. It's just not going to happen. We all come from different backgrounds, have different experiences, and have different expectations and assumptions.

In many cases, signals that may indicate a certain range of emotions to you might that be completely different from somebody else. They might express themselves in a different way.

This is why it's really important to pay attention to the hints that they're sending out when they're talking about certain subjects. If they get **excited**, this means that you're right on the money. There is something about that topic that they truly care about. You might want to keep that in consideration in your efforts at keeping the conversation moving forward and extending it for as long as possible.

By the same token, if somebody was talking about a certain unpleasant topic and they want to ditch the issue as quickly as possible, be on the lookout for this. Be sensitive to these things because you want to extend conversations instead of dwelling on touchy topics that would give that conversation a premature death.

What hints can you really look for? Here is some **low hanging fruit**, so to speak, that you can try to start observing in your daily interactions.

The **excitement**, or lack thereof, in someone's voice when you bring up a topic.

If someone keeps **trying** to bring up a topic, this means they want to talk about it.

If someone keeps looking **away**, this means that they are bored.

If someone's feet are pointed **away** from you, this means they want to stop talking to you.

If you **interrupted** someone right as they were about to speak, ask them about it after you finish speaking to see what direction they were interested in going.

See if you can tell if their smiles and laughs are **fake** or real, depending on how big they are and how quickly they fade or stop.

If someone ignores what you say and goes back to what they were saying **before** you spoke, they feel strongly about their point and want to expand on it.

If someone is **leaning** their head on their hand, this means that they might be bored with the current flow of the conversation.

Look for how strongly someone is nodding in agreement with you, and on the flip side, how little excitement or emotion there is in **reaction**.

Keep the conversation personal.

Even though the person that you're talking to might not be talking **explicitly** about themselves, whatever they are talking about has some sort of **personal significance**. At some level, whatever it is they wish to talk about is important to them – it's inherently personal and somewhat self-serving.

This is why it is extremely important to be present, and observe their signs to figure out what direction they want the conversation to go. By focusing on a **mutually** satisfying subject, you increase the likelihood of a higher level of interaction.

Try to lose yourself in the moment and imagine freestyle dance in conversation form. You feel a certain rhythm from your partner, you **dip** that way. You feel like going another direction, you lead them gently and they follow you knowingly. You can only do this if you are self-aware and observant.

With good enough observation skills like Sherlock Holmes, you can understand how this person thinks, what this person is excited about, and how this person expresses his or herself.

That's what matters because the answers to these questions are what lead to people liking you. Unfortunately, you won't get to this stage if you don't take the time to observe the person. You have to pay attention to the moment and truly understand the emotional components of each and every moment.

<u>Try this exercise:</u>

This is a day of silence! Go out in a public space and sit somewhere where you can watch people in peace. Watch people and their interactions. Can you tell what they are saying without hearing them at all? Can you see which party wants to talk more, and which party is getting bored?

What about if there is attraction, hatred, fakeness, or other hidden emotions that you can observe and pick out? I bet you can, this might be the first time that you have focused entirely on observing others and figuring out what the context is, and outside of your own head.

Chapter 6: Details, details, details.

Rule of Improv Comedy: Provide specific details for people to relate to, react to, and run with.

Great improv comics are great **storytellers**.

A lousy comic just takes a canned **story**, whips it out, and leaves it to the audience members to do whatever they want with it. He recites it like a **lecture** about seahorses, and it's about as engaging as one. It's boring, uninspired, and you can tell that they are just going through the motions and not selling the story.

A great improv comedian, on the other hand, looks at the facial expressions of the crowd and how they react to everything he says. By understanding the emotional atmosphere in the room, the great improv comedian will tell a story based around the emotional engagement of the people in front of them.

And just how do they cater to people's emotional engagement? **With details, details, details**.

Details are how people connect emotionally to situations

and stories, and what make them **reminisce** and feel the pangs of **nostalgia**. It's always the fine details that bring a story to life, like someone's **scent**, or the way a book **feels** in your hand.

Effective storytelling is all about being as specific as you can and being as detailed as you can. When you offer this level of detail and specificity, you put people in a **specific place**. You let them imagine that they are at a certain time and space. This is a huge amount of power because you **are shaping their reality**. You are inviting them to share a fantasy and you have a tremendous amount of power.

Unfortunately, bad conversationalists and bad improv comedians skimp on the details. Instead, they rely on the story alone to deliver the impact. Great storytelling and improv are all about setting the right framework with **intimate** details and telling the story that gets the right **emotional payoffs** from the crowd.

Details provide clues to what is important.

One of the reasons why detailed storytelling is crucial to effective communications is the fact that they clue us in as to what is **important** in the story.

Whenever you are listening to a story you can tell that a particular part of the story is more important than other parts when there's a lot more details regarding that part. This is extremely important because by focusing on what's notable you can direct a story to produce a certain result. Also, the more details regarding what's important, the higher the likelihood the person listening to the story will get the story.

If you want to talk about something, you hint about it with more details that you want people to pick up on. Others will do the same, maybe even **subconsciously**. It's up to you to pay attention to what details you're sending out, and what you might be receiving or missing.

Every story also has a **goal and direction**. It's easy to see where in a well-told story the goal or objectives are. Nine times out of ten, these parts of the story are outlined in more detail. Less important areas aren't.

Details get the reader emotionally invested.

Effective communicators get their audience members **emotionally invested** in what they're doing. They get them to laugh, feel mad, feel sad, or feel surprise – they can control moods, and it's an underrated power.

For example, if you include details about specific **songs** from an era, it's likely that someone will have memories attached to those songs and become more emotionally interested in your story.

Great speakers use details of conversations, jokes and narratives to get people emotionally invested. The opposite of this is when people are just droning on and on and the story is boring, generic and pointless. The person hearing the story feels that there is really no point to the story. This is the kind of conversation that you don't want – **vague and uninteresting**.

It's the difference between someone answering that they went skiing last weekend and thought it was fun, and someone answering that they went skiing last weekend in the mountains and nearly ran over two kids on their way to a record run with their estranged brother. One version is generic and boring, the other is interesting and I **dare** you to not create a conversation from that!

There is no such thing as **TMI – too much information**. Share details about all the figurative nooks and crannies, because that's what makes you interesting on an emotional level.

Try this exercise:

Ask someone to tell you about his or her weekend. If they had a boring weekend, just ask them to tell you about one of their most fun weekends in the past year.

They will probably have a lot to say about it. Covertly, count the number of details that they give to certain parts of the story.

Try asking them to elaborate on the parts of the story where there was more detail. Are they far more excited about talking about those parts? Now try asking them to elaborate on parts of the story where there was little detail. Did they care at all?

You can easily use details to find out what matters to people and what excites them. Let this guide your conversations.

Chapter 7: "No." is a big no-no.

Rule of Improv Comedy: Never lead with "No." because it disregards the direction that someone wants to go and makes it more difficult to work towards a common, shared goal.

Everything you say during improv has an effect.

You might think it doesn't, but that that would be the fallacy of someone that doesn't do well in conversation. Everything has an effect, and it **should**.

If you want to become a great conversationalist, you have to be mindful of the signals you're sending out to others. They all build a big picture and every small detail can make the difference between failure and success. Each signal is a **breadcrumb** in the trail that leads to a great conversation.

If you say "No." in the beginning, you immediately set the wrong **tone** for your interaction. You immediately derail the train **before** it has the opportunity to build up any conversational steam. Why?

If you begin a sentence with the word "No.", you

immediately set a **negative** tone for your interplay with your audience. It becomes doubly difficult for a conversation **flow** to begin and become established. Alternatively, it becomes harder for you to maintain a conversation because you started on a negative foot.

Another downside to starting off with "No." is that it blocks the addition of new **information**. You're basically just saying to that person that no additional information is needed or welcome. You've already made your own decision, and are not interested in listening to their reasons or details.

For example, your friend asks you whether you've seen the basketball game that was going viral online. You simply say "No." and don't show any interest otherwise. What is your friend going to think? That you are just disinterested, and you have just shut down their excitement at showing you something they enjoy. You just seem like you don't care about what they are saying, and minimizes what they want to say. This may be true, but it's not something that you should be open about.

Contrast that with answering **positively**, and letting your friend direct a conversation about the basketball game. It might only take a minute for them to explain or show you exactly what they found so funny, but their mood will be positive after, and you can direct the interaction where you want afterwards.

Also, if you've already started talking to that person and things seem to be going well, the moment you drop "No.", it cancels out all the good feelings and vibes you have previously established. All that stuff that you've already talked about is flipped on its head and you have to start from scratch all over again.

Unfortunately, a lot of people do this **subconsciously**.

They keep using "No." and they are left wondering as to what happened to the conversation. Take the role of the salesperson.

A well-known sales technique is to continue to ask people escalating questions that inevitably they answer "Yes." to, such as "Would you like to save more money?" They thrive on creating a **flow of positivity**, and the positivity leads to sales because people imagine what they are missing. When you begin a sentence with "No." you are essentially poisoning the mind of your prospect as to what's **possible**, for better or worse.

You have to remember that any kind of sales activity involves selling a dream, and saying "No." destroys the possibility of that dream.

It's much easier to talk to somebody in discovery mode compared to damage control mode.

It sends the wrong message.

Nobody really intends to be offended when somebody says the word "No."

On a **conscious** level, we can **intellectually** understand why people would have objections. We can totally understand the concept of every coin having two sides. We're all mature adults, right?

The problem is we're also **emotional** creatures and on an emotional level, the word "No." can be read as combative, hostile, stubborn and **confrontational**. Saying "No." can sometimes be seen as a **rejection** of someone's very identity.

It's very easy to read all sorts of **negative emotions** into sentences that start with the word "No." On one hand, you can be perceived on a subconscious emotional level as hostile and combative. In the best-case scenario, you might be seen as stubborn, hard- headed and close-minded. Neither of these situations is good. This is why it is extremely important for most people to just completely cut out the word "No." when starting off a sentence.

"No" makes people **walk on eggshells** around you. They feel that certain topics are off limits. When people get this impression, conversations don't flow. Conversations become more of a chore rather than a mutually enjoyable process of getting to know each other. It's only a matter of time until they conclude that the benefits of knowing you are **outweighed** by the hassles of having to talk around you and to you at all. It might just be too much of a hassle to try to know you better, and you'll be left hanging alone.

This really is a tragedy because it's all based on a very common misunderstanding. By simply avoiding this practice, you can have more meaningful conversations that can lead to genuine friendships.

Recall that improv comedy is about working towards a

common shared goal. How many productive situations arise when there is a fundamental **disagreement**, and either party feels like they are not being heard?

<u>Try this exercise:</u>

This is a sales technique and exercise. Converse with a friend and try to sell them on a new car. Phrase each sentence into a question that has to make them answer "Yes." such as them saving money or getting more convenience from the car. You should be able to string together at least five such questions.

Now imagine that your friend just says "No." to each of them. Where does that leave you? Probably just speechless, now knowing where to go, and like your entire purpose has been disrupted.

Chapter 8: Don't end up in the same place you started.

Rule of Improv Comedy: Interactions must always be moving ahead, because staying stagnant is death.

I've already told you that one of the secrets to great improv is to never start with fixed idea of what you want to say and when you want to say it. If you do this, you run the risk of **spectacular** failure when you are derailed only a tiny bit. You should only be working with only a rough **framework**, and play the details by ear.

It's also important that you don't have a fixed **destination** in mind, like thinking that an interaction has to resolve one particular issue or you have to get to a particular stance or topic.

That is not effective improv comedy – it is the **open-ended** nature of improv comedy that makes it so engaging and entertaining.

Great improv always leads somewhere. After the improv skit is over, the audience members put their hands together and clap because they feel that they arrived somewhere. They feel a sense of satisfaction and closure because they have moved from **Point A to Point B**, and fulfilled the necessary aspects of a story and journey.

The best improv comedy groups make you feel that there was a **direction** and a purpose to the few hours you spent watching the troupe. It's not a preset place that you end up in, but there's a sense of **closure**. There's a shared feeling that something got done, something got achieved. This is very different from a specific answer or a specific place.

To apply the rules of improv comedy into your efforts at becoming a better conversationalist, there better be a sense of direction and purpose in your conversation.

It has to feel to all people involved that the conversation has gone somewhere meaningful. In other words, some sort of shared positive emotional reaction is evident at the end of the conversation. People don't feel like they are left hanging; there is a **payoff**.

Use the Hero Cycle to your advantage.

One of the famous cultural anthropologists who ever existed is **Joseph Campbell**.

Joseph Campbell was an Ivy League academic who studied the major myths of all the world's major spiritual traditions, and according to Professor Campbell, all these great myths and stories share certain elements in common. Regardless of whom the stories are told to, they are always effective because they hit on certain classic themes. One classic theme that Professor Campbell likes to expound on is the **Hero Cycle**.

Whenever we're talking about Buddha, Jesus Christ, Mohammed, Greek mythology or Hindu mythology, the same elements are at play. The hero of the story starts at point A, and a situation arises that necessitates that the hero go to point B. On the way back from point B to point A, certain conflicts and resolutions occur and the hero is forever transformed.

According to Professor Campbell, people all over the world respond to the Hero Cycle in a very predictable manner because we all **share** these stages in life. We all share these important personal elements that involve growing up, confronting fear, becoming a new person, overcoming adversity and dealing with change.

There's only one thing that is constant in life and that is change. The Hero Cycle goes a long way in explaining how people from all over the world, from all sorts of cultures, class levels and education levels deal with the same **phenomena** in pretty much the same way.

Why am I talking about Professor Campbell and the Hero Cycle here? **Great stories and great conversations are journeys.** They never remain in the same place. There is a sense of direction, there is a sense of conflict that needs resolution, and there is a sense of tension that needs to be unwound.

Real stories draw you in because your own **internal narrative** is put into the play. You can identify with the character that's going from point A to point B. Whatever drama they go through resonates with your own personal drama and issues. Effective conversationalists know this.

This is why they **exaggerate their emotional cues** when telling a story or engaging in a conversation, and they especially exaggerate the **distinct** parts of the Hero Cycle: point A (where they start), what makes them start their journey, conflicts, and how the hero is changed by getting to point B.

You can apply this to any topic of conversation.

Steak, for example. You bring up steak (point A), and then what made you bring up steak on this particular occasion. Then, you talk about how this made you feel differently about steak, or how it has changed you or your view of steak. If you find that you can't apply this to your story about steak, it simply means that your story about steak was mostly pointless.

Another example, you are telling a story about buying **shoes**. You first talk about the current state of your shoes, what made you want to buy new ones, the difficulties you faced in choosing a new pair, and how much better they are compared to your old pair.

Seem unnecessary to apply a **microcosm** of the Hero Journey in each statement or story? It might at first, but then you might start realizing how empty and pointless many of your interactions and conversations were.

The Hero Journey actually gives each statement, assertion, or story you have some meat and something to work from.

<u>Your conversation should be an action movie.</u>

When you go to a movie, you're not really looking for something that fits your daily life.

It's the stuff that's **imperfect and extraordinary** that draws your attention. It's people who are **unusual**, who somewhat **deviate** from the norm that draw your eye.

Keep this in mind when telling a story because it's the unusual elements that are **flavorful**.

Let's face it, if you're going to watch a movie about somebody's life, you wouldn't want to watch the mundane parts where they go to the bathroom and eat toast.

Instead, you want to see the **unique, interesting, and exaggerated** parts. You are looking for high-level conflict. You are looking for the weird events, and by extension, weird characters. You're looking for stuff that breaks away from stagnation and that goes above and beyond the ordinary.

In the same vein, your conversations should be like that. They should be **larger than life**. The great conversations focus on all the things that you could be talking about and filter out the mundane stuff. They focus on the things that get attention.

Even if you work at a library (and presumably live the antithesis of an action movie), you can embody this lesson simply by knowing your personal action scenes. In other words, everyone has something interesting that they've done in the past week or month – just have those things ready and on-hand when people ask how your weekend was.

You can also make your life seem more like an action movie by answering slightly different questions than you were asked. For example, someone asks you "How was your weekend?" Don't take them so literally about the most recent weekend, and instead answer something like "Didn't do much last weekend, but a couple weeks ago my uncle came to visit and brought his pet python! It was ridiculous…"

There are many ways to make sure that your interactions and conversations don't stay **stagnant**. Stagnation is one of the sneakier causes of poor interactions, because it's something that we all do – it's the lazy person's way of conversing, and the lowest effort manner of communication.

Improv is about building **structures** that people can work with, and giving them an emotional **journey** that they can relate to is something that they can't help but respond to.

Try this exercise:

Remember the last story someone told you. What made it a good story, and did you even enjoy it? Now pay attention to the next story someone tells you. Did you like it? Were you emotionally invested?

Sure, it's about delivery. But it's also about the innate emotional value and journey that a story gives you. Did the object of the story go anywhere, and did they change? Did that correlate directly to how much you cared about the story?

Chapter 9: Cultivate entertainment.

Rule of Improv Comedy: Improv is about creating entertaining and interesting situations for the other players and the audience.

When was the last time you remembered somebody you talked to at a dinner party who was extremely **boring**? Probably **never**.

Human beings have minds that are wired to pay attention to things that are noteworthy. The reality of most people's lives is that the vast bulk of our time is spent experiencing things that are very **mundane**. We are talking about stuff like watching grass grow, paint peel or watching the arms slowly move on a wall clock. Do you remember how many times you went to the bathroom today or yesterday? No, because **who cares**?

If you were to ask somebody to tell a story, they would tell stories that are exciting and entertaining, and different from the vast majority of their experiences. There's no point otherwise.

They would tell you about exciting events like getting in a

car accident, surviving a flood or any other personal experience that involves a lot of thrills, chills and spills.

The human brain can only store so much information. This is why it is constantly editing its experiences.

Improv comics know this – that's why they seek to create **entertaining** situations in each performance. Otherwise, why would their audience care to watch them at all? Otherwise, why would they the players do improv at all if they weren't entertained by doing it?

Improv comedy is focused on entertaining everyone involved and watching.

Great entertainment has a high degree of emotional engagement. Keep this in mind because improv comedy techniques help you become a better conversationalist if you are able to bring a lot of entertainment in your conversations.

Keep in mind that people talk to other people for three main reasons. Either they are looking for entertainment, pleasure, or general information and utility. If you were to choose among these three reasons, **choose entertainment**. Why? You might be a walking encyclopedia, but you can also be entirely forgettable if you focus on simply sharing information or dishing out useful information.

If they are looking for entertainment, nothing is more entertaining than having another flesh and blood **human being** in front of you with different tones of voice, facial expressions and gestures and body language. Sure, you could pop a DVD into your DVD player and watch an entertaining show. But live entertainment is much different because it is very easy for you to get emotionally pulled in to the conversation. You are not just a **passive** observer or audience. You actually become part of the **narrative**. There is a back and forth call and response dynamic that turns face-to-face conversations into one of the most **vibrant** and in-depth types of human communication you would ever engage in.

Don't **squander** the potential of the entertainment that you can offer and receive from conversations!

Here are some tips that you need to keep in mind when using entertainment to become a better conversationalist.

Don't take it so seriously.

The key to entertaining conversations is that they do not take themselves so seriously that the focus becomes an **intellectual pissing match**. You are not there to prove anything. You are there simply to get people to enjoy being around you.

These are two totally different goals. People who give **speeches** or talk to other people with a set agenda tend to become serious because they want to achieve something. This tends to strip the life out of the things and instead of something vibrant and enjoyable, it can easily become dry or one sided.

There is definitely a time and place for this type of speech. However, if you are simply trying to master the art of conversation and want to become a more entertaining and fun person to be around, don't take things too seriously.

The key here is **mutual enjoyment**. Do not feel that you are lecturing somebody or proving something to somebody because eventually they would not longer feel that it is fun. They would no longer feel that the experience is enjoyable. In many cases, they might equate you with a boring professor or academic. A more common scenario is that they just don't like you, and don't want to talk to you.

Envision that the goal and entire purpose of your conversation is to make the other person **laugh**, feel **good**, and perhaps feel **special** by the amount of interest and enthusiasm you show in them.

Be the first to lighten the mood by throwing in a joke – even an obviously lame one can let people know that you want to loosen things up, and sometimes this is relieving for people.

The more pressure you put on your conversation, the more serious and strained it becomes.

Move past generic topics.

One of the key skills you need to learn in being an entertaining conversationalist is your ability to sidestep **boring or generic topics**.

It is very easy to go down a slippery slope where you end up talking about something that is highly academic, highly technical or otherwise lifeless and boring. Eventually, the conversation grinds to a halt. In many cases, you only realize that you have gone down that slippery slope when it is too late.

Instead, focus on thinking **outside the box**. Focus on throwing little **spice nuggets** out there to change the direction of the conversation to something more fun, provocative or controversial.

Great communicators are always looking for vivid emotional signals from people they are talking to, so they can control and manipulate the conversation to a place where people remain engaged.

Again, the goal is not to inform somebody. The goal is not to lay out a package of information. Instead, the goal is to get people to walk away with a feeling that you are worth knowing. Give people the impression that you are fun to know. This is the difference between entertainment and educational talks.

How can you spice up a conversation?

Play Devil's advocate. Compare something to a Disney movie plot. Ask personal questions. Answer to questions in movie or song quotes. Completely change topics. Think out loud about questions you have about life. Ask hypothetical questions based on what you see around you.

It's easy once you get into the state of mind to treat your conversations as entertainment.

If you find yourself caught in a **slow avalanche** of boring questions and queries, don't be afraid to simply proclaim "Hold on, **why** are we talking about work outside of work? I want to hear all about the crazy times you've been having with your **new girlfriend**!" This isn't going to hurt anyone's feelings, because even if they wanted to talk about work, they want to talk even more about their personal life and new girlfriend.

<u>Don't be afraid to "go there".</u>

One of the most common ways people kill their conversation is when they feel that they have to walk on **eggshells** and **filter** themselves on many topics.

The problem with this approach is it eats up so much of your energy that it saps your ability to come up with interesting twists to the conversation to keep the conversation going. You eventually tire yourself out trying to **dance** around people's sensitivities that your conversation dies an **early death**. **Safe is boring**.

The solution to this is actually to just look at the sensitive areas or topics straight in the eye. **Don't be afraid to go there**.

At the very least, people will give you **grudging respect** because you would talk about things that they do not normally talk about. You'll be memorable for your **chutzpah**. You will stand out from the rest of the crowd that spends all this time, effort and energy dancing around certain topics.

By and large, people are just oversensitive these days...

more accurately, people think **others** are oversensitive.

In my line of work, I get asked sensitive questions all the time. 100% of the time when I am asked "I hope you don't mind me asking..." **I never care**.

It's never really that sensitive of a topic, I don't mind being open with others, and it's never prying into a dungeon of my life that I don't want exposed. Most people think this way, so don't be afraid to ask about things that you would hesitate to otherwise.

Personal life and relationships? People love talking about this with others, if only to brag.

People's stances on controversial or sensitive topics? As long as you don't argue and debate them endlessly, people love the chance to expound on their beliefs.

Their unfiltered opinions on people and things? Everyone loves a good bitching or rant, even if they won't admit it.

<u>Don't hide your personality.</u>

The final way to ensure that your conversation is boring is to become a **safe** version of yourself. You hide your personality because you aren't sure how you are going to be taken, how people will react to you, and how much people will like the true you.

But that's totally bunk. People are talking to you **because** they think you are different. They think you have something different to contribute. If they just wanted the same observation or the same take as everybody else, they'd talk to anyone else.

Let your **quirks** and personality show. They will draw people to you who really enjoy you, and push away those who don't. Why would you want to be surrounded by those that don't just understand your quirks? It's freeing, empowering, and a hell of a lot more entertaining to be yourself and bounce your personality off those who are like-minded.

Never be afraid to put your personality on center stage because that is the **only** thing differentiating you from the vast herd of people out there.

Strive to loosen up and just treat your conversations as an exercise in creating a fun environment – how fun and absurd can you make it?

Try this exercise:

Sit a friend down and tell them to prepare for fun. Ask them all the questions that you never dared to ask. Sex. Relationships. Sex. Politics. Religion. Family. Sex. Fears. Flaws.

What kind of conversation follows every time you ask one of those questions? People share their stances. And it becomes impossible not to have an interesting discourse about those stances, how they reconcile with yours, and how they came to embrace those stances.

People are open to more topics than you think, and often have a lot to say on them, which encourages a great conversation.

Chapter 10: It's in the name – improvise!

Rule of Improv Comedy: Great improv is a result of the creativity in spontaneous situations, and set agendas and outlines put a very low ceiling on that.

Improv players can occasionally work with a set **theme** between the players themselves, but improv inevitably involves a lot of crowd and audience work. That's part of the fun in attending an improv show – you feel that you are a **part** of the outcome and have contributed to the show.

Great improv comedians work the crowd instead of being worked by the crowd. They do this precisely because they **improvise**, and don't have some sort of template or some sort of pre-planned program. You can't predict what a crowd will give you to work with, so it's out of **necessity** that they can't have an agenda or outline.

Improv comedy is all about reading signals that others send you, working with those signals, and then reflecting them right back. Improv comedy is **collaborative** in nature. It becomes some sort of intimate conversation that an improv comic has with an audience.

How does knowing all this make you a better conversationalist?

Professional improv players are able to create a fluid and dynamic and witty interplay with their audience members because they are **flexible** and open to any possibility and direction. The first step is to let go of any preconceived notion of how and where you want an interaction to go. It can be a little **scary** to go into something feeling unprepared, but it can actually be very freeing to realize that you can do it easily.

And you won't be completely unprepared. The broad strokes and major themes you might want to cover, those can be there and planned.

The secret to starting and maintaining great conversations is to learn to have **broad outlines**, then **adapt** to the person you are talking to. This is thinking on your feet and improvising.

Agendas make people suspicious.

You have to remember that when you talk to other people, the focus of the conversation should be about **the conversation**. It should not be about what you want and it is not about your agenda or what you are trying to get out of the other person.

The moment other people are able to perceive this, guess what will happen? They will shut you out. You instantly become somebody worthy of **suspicion and skepticism**. If you are trying to sell something, it makes it all that much harder once people feel that you have an agenda. It's difficult to overcome the feeling that someone wants something from you.

This is why it is extremely important to constantly listen to other people and acknowledge them. Let them feel that they are helping set the agenda. Let them feel that the conversation really is a two-way street. And it actually becomes a two-way street when you stop and listen to them. People like to be made to feel that they matter.

If you want to develop better relationships and become a more effective conversationalist and leader, you need to get people to feel that you listened to them. The best way to do this is, of course, to actually do it.

Consider the alternative.

The **alternative**, of course, is having an **agenda** for a conversation. There are a few drawbacks.

First, it becomes exceedingly clear that you are only waiting for your turn to speak, and not actually listening to people.

People might say something to you, and you might not even acknowledge their statement, and just continue along with yours. Others will notice your patterns sooner than you think, and eventually just **stop** talking to you. What are they getting out of a conversation like that?

Second, entering a conversation with a fixed agenda is that you eventually get **lost** if you deviate from the agenda in the slightest bit. This is bound to happen if you engage in real conversations. Unless you are just going to drop a speech on somebody, things will never go exactly as you plan it.

And when you create an agenda, you memorize it and become **reliant** on it. What happens when you deviate and can't find a good place to step back into your agenda? You're left utterly unprepared for the rest of the interaction because of your agenda reliance.

When you set **flexible talking points**, you at least give yourself some sort of large boundary area with which to work with. This gives you a sense of control in how you are going to hold up your end of the conversation. At the very least, it gives some sort of shape and direction to what would otherwise be a free-for-all conversation. This is very different from having a very fixed set agenda that dictates the direction of the conversation.

Appearing controlling.

Another downside to having a fixed agenda is that it is very easy to come off as **controlling**.

It is very easy to be confused as somebody who is out to **dominate** the conversation, or worse, have some sort of ulterior motive. This is a serious problem because even if you do not have an **ulterior motive**, simply having an agenda makes you seem like you do. Since most people do not like to feel that they are manipulated, controlled or otherwise tricked, things can get quite negative very quickly.

With that said, having an agenda in an online conversation is easier than pursuing an agenda in a face-to-face conversation. Since you are communicating using e-mail or online chat, it is easier for you to pursue elements of your agenda and not turn off the person you are communicating with. This is very hard to do when you are actually just talking to the person on a face-to-face basis.

The death of spontaneity.

So much of the beauty in our lives is **unplanned**. It's because we are able to step outside of the boxes and **limits** in our heads, and explore things we wouldn't have otherwise. And what results is often amazing.

If you are looking for yet another reason why you should not have a fixed agenda when talking to people, a fixed agenda **kills spontaneity**. It is like a **straitjacket** for your conversation.

When you remove the possibility of spontaneity from your conversations, you might feel like you are safe from spectacular **failure**. That might be true, but you also **limit** the potential of where your conversation can go.

Real conversations do not really have a fixed destination. It is not about changing somebody's mind, it is not about making the best impression or necessarily winning somebody over. It is simply just an exercise of getting to know each other and connect.

Try this exercise:

This is about practicing working and talking without a set agenda. Hopefully it will help you realize that you don't need one, and that your worst-case scenario is not really that bad.

Pick five topics that you know absolutely nothing about. Bring them up one by one with a friend. Talk for each topic for at least 5 minutes. See the various angles and routes you can go to making a topic interesting. Grasp for straws on how to keep a dialogue going. Notably, see how you can relate it to other topics, and see how easy it is to get sidetracked onto something else.

Chapter 11: Make everyone else look good.

Rule of Improv Comedy: Since you are all working towards a shared goal, you are everyone else's supporting actor so do your best to make your fellow improv players look good and they will do the same to you.

Conversations are all about getting to feel that you know each other better – that's the shared goal.

It all boils down to **likability**. One of the most effective ways to get people to like you is to make **them** look good in your conversation. When you make them feel like **heroes**, it is easier for them to like you in return.

People like those that are like them.

One of the secrets of highly effective salespeople is to **mirror** their prospects.

Maybe their prospects have certain body gestures, or talk at a certain speed or in a certain way. Expert sales people would mirror certain elements of their prospect's persona.

Highly effective sales people are able to close sale after sale because they are able to exploit one fundamental **human weakness**.

People like other people who are like them. We tend to like people who look like us, act like us, talk like us, sound like us and do things like us. This should not be a surprise. If you were to hop on a time machine and go back thousands of years in human evolution, you would realize that people tended to cluster around other people that look like them.

If you were very welcoming of others that are very different from them, chances are you probably would not too long. There is an evolutionary advantage to clustering with people that are similar to us. While humanity has changed dramatically over 50,000 years, our minds are still hardwired to reward people that are like us.

For purpose of illustration, say you were born in a small town in Alaska. How would you feel to meet someone also from that small town? Wouldn't you automatically like them more and think more highly of them?

Seek to mirror people's body language, rate of speech, mannerisms. Also seek to find the commonalities (both shallow and deep) that you share with someone as soon as possible, so you can share an implied bond.

Be an amazing supporting actor.

One of the easiest ways to do this is to shine the **spotlight** on them. Make their actions look more dramatic and decisive than they really are.

By overemphasizing your conversation partner's **importance**, you increase their perceived value to others. This gives them a tremendous reason to like you. It all boils down to you making it easier your conversation partner to shine.

One of the most common ways to do this is to ask for their opinion and lay out some facts that support that opinion. In other words, this way they look like a genius in front of an audience. Why is this effective?

First, you are going out of your way to make somebody look good. Deep down they feel that you truly get them. At the very least, they feel that they can always come to you for **support**. You are their **fan club**, so to speak.

Another reason is that they can look at you as an **ally**.

They can see you as a source of personal influence and support. You become a safe bet for them to keep coming back to for **validation**. You have to remember that we often have a lot of critics surrounding us. When we spot one or two supporters, it is human nature for us to seek out these supporters and feel comfortable around them. They become our centers of refuge and comfort.

For example, if you know that someone likes talking about ancient Greece, shine the spotlight on them in a related conversation by saying "Hey John, isn't this something that you studied a lot? I bet you have an opinion on this phenomena."

You can also ask for the **recommendations** and then explain why that recommendation makes a lot of sense.

For example, "Thanks for that insight, that makes a lot of sense. I never thought about ski lodges that way before."

Finally, you can direct the conversation to topics that **they** are knowledgeable about, and let them share their expertise with you.

If it is obvious that you are just trying to flatter this person, butter them up or blow smoke up their butts, you are creating more problems than you are solving. That's why these tactics are much better than simply praising or complimenting them. That gets old, and gets transparent very quickly.

There's nothing manipulative about being a **great supporting actor**. You're not just telling them things to make them happy. You are just finding the **golden nuggets** within everyone and bringing them to the light so that they can sparkle.

Try this exercise:

Sit a friend down. Bring up only topics that they are knowledgeable in and like to talk about. Ask them relevant questions about it, and make clear that you are asking them because of their expertise.

How much do you think they are going to love that conversation? You might not say more than 100 words, but they'll think it was amazing because they got to get on their soapbox and expound on their inner workings, and everyone loves doing that.

Chapter 12: Remember and reincorporate details from earlier.

Rule of Improv Comedy: Reincorporate specific elements from earlier in the interaction in different contexts for big laughs.

The funny thing about great stories is that nine times out of ten, they involve some sort of **recycling**.

I don't mean recycling in the sense that elements are just repeated and re-used from other stories, but rather that there are certain aspects that are repeated over and over to emphasize specific **emotional high points**. These are often what end up making a story great. Each time a specific element is re-visited, the point just grows **stronger**, and the laughs get bigger.

Even great artists will often recycle certain elements from the same piece of work. It's **not** for lack of creativity or imagination, it's simply to deliver the message in a stronger manner, and **emphasize** specific points. This happens repeatedly in literature, for example, when an author continues to bring up a character's background or love of a particular brand of whiskey – you know that it **foreshadows** some importance later in the story.

Talented improv comics know how to recycle specific elements in such a way that it adds to the story and gets huge laughs, just because suddenly two elements (the old one and the current one) are tied together.

The elements often don't appear to work together at all until the comic links them together, and the combination is often hilarious. As a result, the comic automatically appears intelligent, observant, and extremely witty for having linked them.

This is not a chapter about simply saying the same thing over and over again, nor about sticking to patterns of conversation that have worked in the past.

It's to reincorporate past elements into the current topic of conversation in a way that shows observation and wit. If you notice that a lot of your conversations tend to repeat over and over until people you are talking to lose interest, you would do well to pay close attention to this chapter.

The art of properly reincorporating elements from earlier in a conversation can be easy once you understand how and why it works.

Why reincorporate?

When you repeat an element that you and your conversation partner talked about earlier, this shows to that person in no uncertain terms that you were **listening** to that person.

This drives home the point that whatever they said is **important** enough to you for you to take notice and act on. This is important because as I mentioned earlier, the whole point of conversation is to get people to like you, feel good about you, and relax and open up to you.

When you repeat certain themes or elements from an earlier point of the conversation, you show your conversation partner that you are very observant and actually care about the conversation. This is important because it brings home the point that they matter to you, that they are important enough to you to pay attention to and repeat.

Create inside jokes.

When you reincorporate something that somebody said, not only do they feel that they matter, but they feel that you share something in common with them. There was something that happened between you two that only you two can refer to.

When you repeat that element, it serves as a reference point for **humor**, shared wit and otherwise a point of good feeling. It is as if you reached a point in your conversation where you saw eye to eye, and that's **literally** a moment that no one else can share in.

This is a tremendous benefit because in today's world, it is very easy to feel alienated and separated from others. It is very easy to feel that everybody else is a **stranger**. When you talk to somebody and you have a point in the conversation where you saw each other eye to eye, it makes your conversation partner feel more open to you.

The barrier we all have separating us from everybody else becomes all that much weaker because you were able to create a **bonding** moment based on your particular interaction that suddenly becomes personal and literally **unique**.

Control.

When you reincorporate or repeat certain elements from earlier points of the conversation, this gives you power to **redirect** the conversation as you please. If you wanted to go back to that earlier point, you can now easily segue into it.

It lends an air of **familiarity** to a conversation by confining it to something that you have already talked about. This gives you the best of both worlds. It allows you to keep the conversation from dragging by introducing something new. However, it is also talking about something fairly familiar so that the new direction is not seen as a **threat** or some sort of completely off topic direction.

Counter intuitively, this **repetition** can save your conversation from becoming long drawn out and boring. It lets them know that you actually take whatever they are saying seriously. By being observant, you place proper importance to their impressions and the content that they shared. This can help further the bond that you have with that person.

Finally, it's just funny.

This whole chapter has probably been slightly abstract and nebulous for some. Without **examples**, all this chapter says to do is to bring up earlier points that were funny or powerful, and integrate them into the current topic.

That's essentially it, but the impact and humor this can make is best illustrated through example.

You are talking with a friend about **puppies**, and you discover that your friend has never actually held a live puppy, just marveled at them from a distance. This is probably going to constitute a high point, because it's something that is slightly shocking, and funny when you think about it. This is something that you might want to reincorporate.

Later in the conversation, the topic turns to **rollercoasters**, and specifically how your friend loves them. How do you reincorporate the part about puppies?

It's just combining the two elements in a **novel** way. "I guess you spent all of your time on rollercoasters and ignored the cute puppies in the amusement parks..."

Another example: you are talking about coffee and you divulge that you hate it. Consider that a conversational high point. Then the topic turns to the cleanliness of public bathrooms. You could reincorporate the earlier high point by making a comment about how you are safe from public bathrooms because don't drink coffee (coffee is a diuretic and makes you have to urinate).

<u>Try this exercise:</u>

Have a conversation with a friend, but have a pen and paper in hand. Try to note conversational high points when they happen, and write them down for reference later. Then, write down all of the topics as they come up.

Take all of the conversational high points you listed, and see how you can combine them with the subsequent topics that arose like in the example above. This may seem like an odd exercise, but this is exactly what thinking on your feet is – except now you get to practice it.

Chapter 13: Yes, we are talking about practice.

Rule of Improv Comedy: There's a reason why the people involved in improv comedy are called players and why performances are treated like sports games – it's something that people practice for, to produce the best result like any sport.

I've laid out some solid guidelines and techniques for conversation mastery in this book. Just **don't** expect these rules to pay off immediately.

There are some things you can put into practice immediately... but ultimately, you have to understand that for you to get truly good at anything, you have to **practice, practice and practice**.

Excellence does not happen **overnight**. Everything that is worth anything must be trained, and must be worked on. It is like a sport. It takes practice and sometimes takes a while to see visible improvement.

What do improv players have to **practice**?

Timing, reaction to others, how to deal with certain

situations and topics, what their comfort zones are, what they are good at, what they are bad at, reading other people… they can literally never practice enough because there are so many variables in human interaction.

So what makes you think that **conversation**, which involves all of those same elements, would be so easy?

You also have to remember that just because you stepped up to the plate does not necessarily mean you are going to hit the ball. In many cases, you have to strike out before you hit a home run. You have to pay your dues and the same applies to great conversation skills.

The power of momentum.

If there is any saving grace in the trying process of improving your conversational skills with improv, it is this: eventually you will reach your point of **momentum**.

This means that by simply repeating an action over and over again, you set in motion a series of steps that paves the way to success. It is all about getting up and trying again and again, and sooner or later you will realize that it's been a while since you've fallen down. This will instill additional confidence in you, and confidence is a **key** component of skills.

This is what separates people that become great conversationalists from people that simply throw in the towel.

There is nothing fundamentally **wrong** with people who are bad conversationalists. They have the same hardware as you. They have the same capacity for excellence. They only lack one thing. They do not want to try or they tried and tried, failed and they do not want to try again. They experience discomfort, unfamiliarity, and awkwardness and decide that they **can't** take it anymore and don't want to face it.

You have to learn how to recover from your mistakes and learn from your mistakes. You have to keep in mind that what separates losers from winners is that winners know that success means having to get back up. After all, what are the **real** negative consequences here? Feeling awkward and embarrassed for a couple of minutes? That's a very small price to pay to unlock the conversation skills that can literally change your life.

Losers on the other hand throw in the towel, they quit and they call it a day. The only way to lose is to quit. As long as there is time left on the clock, you can still make the shot.

You have to always remember that not everything will go as planned, but if you **constantly** practice and you constantly put yourself in a position to learn, eventually you will reach that momentum point.

Mastery does **not** happen overnight. Whether we are talking about making more money, becoming a more confident person or a more effective speaker or conversationalist, it simply does not happen overnight. It is not like a product you go to the store, pick up off a shelf and check out.

The conversation skills that I am teaching you help you become a better communicator because they help you change from within. They change the way you talk to people, they change the way you value people and your **relationships** with people. Nine times out of ten, external change can only happen after internal change has taken place.

This is why you need to be patient. Just as you want to be become a better conversationalist, this also involves you becoming more in tune with your own feelings and be more respectful of the feelings of others.

Skill acquisition.

Just like with any other kind of skill that you are trying to improve, **skill improvement** does not always go as planned. The more you practice your skill, the higher the likelihood that you will get to the next level. However, as I have mentioned, it cannot be planned for.

What you can plan is the amount of time, effort and energy you put into honing your skills.

You have to give yourself the time to hone your skills. This is especially true if you are trying to learn a completely new skill set. You can start out really poorly, but you can get good at it as long as you give yourself the time to practice. Just look at your conversation skills as another skill set.

If you can improve the way you shoot a basketball, you can improve your conversation skills. It is just a matter of time, effort and how badly you want it.

Malcolm Gladwell preached the value of the 10,000-hour rule, which means that it generally takes 10,000 hours of practice to master a skill. It's a process, and there's no shortcut. Where are you in that process?

<u>Intentionality and Immediate feedback.</u>

The biggest and most underrated element for making practice productive is the **immediate feedback** you can receive during it.

That's the only way to know that you are off-course, and how you can steer back into the correct and optimal way of doing things.

That's the problem with the practice habits of many people. They are not **intentional** about what they are doing, and end up just doing the same thing over and over. That's not productive practice, and will mostly serve to reinforce **bad habits**.

People need to embrace intentionality, and know exactly what they are doing and what they should be working on when they practice. This becomes much easier with a practice and accountability partner, and preferably one that knows what you are working on.

It's also the only way that you can receive immediate feedback, which is important because the more delayed feedback is from the actual practice, the less effective it is. People forget what they were working on, and they can't tell the difference from the correct way and the way they were used to. Seeing the **immediate improvement** makes all the difference in making practice stick in someone's head.

For example, you're trying to learn how to shoot a basketball. What's more helpful, a coach being present to see you shoot, and immediately make changes to your form and make sure that you adhere to them? Or for a coach to listen to you talk about your form, and try to make changes verbally a week later?

Try this exercise:

Hey, hasn't this book had a lot of exercise for you to practice your social and conversational skills with? There's no exercise to practice more than to just do it!

Chapter 14: Sometimes you just need to shut up.

Rule of Improv Comedy: Improv comedy is about playing off others, and you can't do that if you are constantly waiting for your turn to talk and not listening to others. Sometimes you just need to shut up and listen patiently.

Have you ever had a conversation with someone, where **immediately** after you finished speaking, they ignored what you said and simply continued their thought? It's as if they didn't hear a word of what you said, and they probably **didn't**.

Real conversations are two-way streets, and you have to **give space** in order to receive it. In many cases, simply receiving or listening is a form of communication. Simply being there is a form of communication.

Unfortunately, for people with bad conversation skills, they look at conversation as a **dumping ground**. This will happens one of two ways.

They will either come in with a fixed **agenda** and a set of talking points, or they will simply be so **wrapped up** in their own lives that they just want to share it with you and not hear about yours. In either case, they then open their mouths, unload all this information and don't stop talking until they get tired of their own voices.

How does this make the **other** person feel? They get the distinct feeling that the other person is just waiting for their turn to speak, and are not interested in **anything** they have to say.

They are really not getting much out of the exchange, and at some point just listening to someone and having your prompts ignored is burdensome and flat-out **annoying**.

To master the art of conversation, understand that silence is an effective communications tool. Use it **frequently**.

In many cases, by simply **shutting up** gives the other person a lot of motivation to talk. You help them push the conversation forward and make them feel comfortable around you.

Don't just wait for your turn to speak.

If you are letting the other person talk and talk simply because you are just waiting for your turn to speak, you are not participating in a **conversation**.

Worse, you are not **respecting** them. It tells them that you do not value them enough to listen to them while you are waiting for your turn to unload what it is you have to say.

True conversation that improves relationships and makes people feel really good about each other and make them feel familiar around each other involves an **interplay** between silence and speaking, and both parties have an equal opportunity to take the spotlight.

Silence by itself can be very positive because if you pair it with active listening, you can increase the amount of personal bonding you have with the person you are talking to. Unfortunately, this is almost **impossible** if you are just simply waiting for that other person to shut up so you can speak. You are just waiting for a break for you to unload what it is you have to say. This leads to all sorts of **bad habits** like interrupting, talking over the person or negating what that person has to say.

Great improv comics are able to kill crowds over and over again because they know when to shut up, use silence to their advantage, and when to pick up cues from the crowd.

It is all about reading the crowd's communications and collaborating with them. Unfortunately, you are not collaborating with your conversation partner if you are just simply waiting for them to shut up. If you are simply waiting for your turn to speak, you are not working on creating an environment where you feel that both of you are bonding and feeling good about each other. This is the complete opposite of a real conversation, and you had better **lower** your expectations for the kind of connection that you are going to create.

Bottom line: people don't like **not** being heard.

No interrupting.

If you interrupt somebody, it is a form of **disrespect**.

What you are just telling that person is whatever you said does **not** matter, and that whatever half-baked thought you had matters far more.

Interrupting somebody sends many different signals, and they are almost all **negative**. It is not just you talking over that person or cutting them off. It sends an important signal regarding respect and value.

When you interrupt somebody, you are basically trying to **dominate** that person. You are trying to devalue what they say. You are also trying to impose your agenda on that person.

You are telling them, "I am the only person is this conversation that is worth listening to and I am the only one that matters." This is the worst form of insult and disrespect. You might think it is not that big of a deal, but if you keep interrupting, that is precisely the kind of signal you are sending.

Obviously, you are not **consciously** trying to do that, and you probably don't mean any ill will when you do it. But that's what's going on inside of your head, and your conversation partner **doesn't** know that. Your actions will say something far worse than your intentions, and you have to realize that there is often a **disconnect** between them.

Really, just don't interrupt others unless you agree with them so emphatically that you can finish their sentence for them. And if you do, ask them immediately after you finish speaking what they were saying before you interrupted them.

In fact, let's institute a **2 second rule**. After someone finishes saying their piece, pause a full 2 seconds while thinking about what they said, and demonstrating that you are contemplating it. Then reply. This will make it appear as if you have truly considered their thoughts and are composing an equally thoughtful response.

Listening and proper reaction.

Great improv works when people actually take the time to listen to feedback, process it carefully and then **react** to it the right way. The emphasis here is on actually **acknowledging** it, and giving them a reaction that lets them know that you have heard their specific statement and not just a "Uh huh" or "Oh I see…"

The same goes with your conversation skills. For you to become a really good conversationalist, you need to learn when to stop talking, listen to what others are saying, properly digest it, and then express the right **reaction**.

This is impossible to do if you refuse to listen to people. They will catch on and they will stop talking to you.

So it's not actually enough to **just** shut up. Staring blankly at someone will make people feel like they have to repeat themselves, and like their message didn't get through – the same exact effect as not listening to them.

You have to be **in** the conversation. This does not just mean being physically there. You have to be mentally and emotionally there as well, and **display** that physically. This is how people feel respected, valued, and heard.

Use your facial expressions, eyebrows, gestures, and laughs to signal a reaction to each of their statements. Nod when they emphasize a point. Encourage them to continue speaking with a "Go on..." Make it clear that what they are saying has affected you.

Conversations are a team activity.

People who are simply looking to be heard are **users**, with few exceptions. These are people that are simply **self-absorbed** and use others for their ears.

It is all about **them**. It is all about their agenda. It is all about what is important to them. There is no space for the other person you are talking to.

Real conversations are all about talking about things that matter to you **equally**. Unfortunately, if you look at conversations as simply just an exercise to be heard and shine a spotlight on your **ego**, you are doing a great disservice to the person you are talking to. Eventually that person will stop talking to you as they are not getting anything out of the conversation. Not everyone is interested in **your** life as you are.

When was the last time you asked how someone's day was, versus just spilling endlessly about your life? When was the last time you really dug deep and tried to learn as much as possible about the person across from you?

If you want to become a better conversationalist, you need to learn when to shut up. As the old saying goes, you only learn when your mouth is shut. The great conversations are all about learning and teaching others.

By giving yourself the opportunity to listen instead of simply waiting for your turn to speak, you put yourself in a position to truly connect with that person. Real conversations are all about real connections. Unfortunately, simply waiting to say what you have to say doesn't get you there, and makes you fundamentally unlikable.

Try this exercise:

Make your next conversation with a friend all about them. Try to find out about every minute detail of their day. This means you shutting up, listening to them, reacting accordingly, and asking questions that go deeper. Say as little as you can while reacting properly, and moving the conversation along to whatever direction they want.

Don't interrupt them, and try to coax at least 5 stories out of them. Note how difficult this is for you to do initially, yet how willing they are to talk about themselves in detail. Did it feel unnatural to ask people deeply about their day? If it did, then you probably had the problem of not being able to shut up.

Chapter 15: If all else fails, just keep HPM in mind.

Rule of Improv Comedy: If all else fails, talk about history, philosophy, or metaphor.

One of the most **powerful** techniques you can adopt from improv comedy is **HPM**.

Conversations tend to hit rough spots that can easily spiral out of control. These rough spots can lead to dead ends that can kill the conversation. Sometimes all the energy and vibrancy of the conversation can evaporate almost instantaneously.

This is why you need to think in terms of HPM.

HPM is like a mental template you can use to put a **creative spin** on your conversation, and you can use it in the best and worst of situations. It's a concept that can apply to **any** topic, **anytime**... and best of all, it does not matter how intelligent or creative both you and the people you are speaking with are. Anyone can do it, as they involve things that everyone has – **opinions** and **personal memories**.

They are **shortcuts** you can take that are short to put an interesting spin into the conversation, so it can kick start it with a renewed energy level. Your proper usage of HPM can mean the difference between your conversation crashing and burning or kicked into a higher gear. With the proper timing and usage of HPM elements, you can keep kick starting your conversation until you talk to that person for **hours** on end.

If you want to have better, more personal, and more vibrant conversations, just remember **HPM**.

What is HPM?

HPM stands for **history, philosophy and metaphor.**

These are multiple angles that you can take with any kind of conversation to add renewed life to a conversation. You can address the history, philosophy, or metaphor of almost anything that was just said.

By using these techniques, you can jump start your conversation and add a higher energy level to it. It is all about timing and using the proper angle.

The best part about each component of HPM is that they are **universal**, and are incredibly fertile grounds for conversation. Everyone has an HPM on just about every topic, and just by saying it loud you galvanize others to bring up their own HPM.

History.

The history angle is when you talk about what your

conversation partner said in a **personal** way and relate it back to something that happened to you – **your personal history**.

For example, if your conversation partner talks about how he lost his sunglasses after going on a rollercoaster, how can you relate that to yourself?

"I hate rollercoasters now, I can't believe I lost my $250 sunglasses last time I went on one!"

There are **three** topics that you can address with your personal history – sunglasses, rollercoasters, and losing things.

Accordingly, your response that invokes your personal history might be something like "Yeah, I remember the last time I went on a rollercoaster, I almost threw up because it was so intense!"

Or, "That reminds me of the time a monkey stole my sunglasses in Bali. I think we need straps for our sunglasses."

Or, "That stinks, I lost my favorite hat last week too. The sun is our enemy now."

The history angle draws its power from the fact that there is **personal involvement**. If somebody uses this technique on you, you cannot help but feel more open and emotionally bonded to that person. Your experience resonated with them in a deep and personal way; you share something!

It got them to think about certain things that happened in their past that have something to do with what you just said. In other words, the history angle **necessitates** a certain amount of opening up.

One word of **caution**: you need to be careful because you do not want to diminish the personal importance of your conversation partner's story. If they were telling you about the time they lost a very valued pet or family member, you do not want to come up with a story that **trivializes** it.

For example, somebody talked about losing their pet dog of 18 years and you compared it with the time you lost your favorite Michael Jordan shoe. It does not even compare, and your personal history is **not** an appropriate response there.

Make sure when you use the history angle to pay close attention to **emotional equivalency and resonance.** If they are very emotionally worked up about something, make sure that your historical comparison is similar. The **impact** must be at the same level, otherwise it is not going to come off favorably.

One more example of how to use personal history in replying to others:

"I love watching soccer, it's definitely my favorite sport to watch!"

"Yeah, I used to play soccer as a kid and actually broke my leg from it, but I like watching too."

Philosophy.

By philosophy, I am not talking about an abstract theoretical argument about what life is.

I am talking about personal philosophy, beliefs, and **opinions**. The philosophy angle is where you demonstrate **how** you feel about something, for better or worse. The **stronger** you feel about something, the more this engenders additional conversation.

We can use the same example from before – someone losing their sunglasses after going on a rollercoaster.

Your philosophy angle response would be something akin to "Oh my God, losing things and the tiny probability of dying on a rollercoaster are why I hate them. I get my adrenaline kicks elsewhere!"

Or, "That's why I'm a believer in cheap, crappy sunglasses. They get the job done."

Or, "I'm deathly afraid of rollercoasters, I'm so amazed by anyone that goes on them."

It brings home the point that this person is actually paying attention to the other person, regardless of whether it **reinforces** their statement or **disagrees** with it.

What that person said resonated with this person enough to share their philosophy and opinion on something. This is **intimate** and it is not hard for the person who made the statement you are commenting on to feel drawn to you for opening up that way.

When you comment on your conversation partner's statement in an **opinionated** way, it is deeply philosophical and personal way, you make a strong personal connection.

However, you can cheapen this and send the wrong signal by being **overly emotional** about everything.

If every topic that that person brings up is met with this highly **visceral** emotional reaction, then you cheapen your emotional reaction. It makes you look like a fool because it would seem that you get emotionally worked up about everything. Instead of making the person you are talking to feel special and valued, it would not be unexpected for them to feel used and **manipulated**.

Metaphor.

When you throw out a metaphor, you communicate with the person you are talking to that you are both emotionally and intellectually **engaged**.

For you to come up with a metaphor it means that you really thought about what they said and you relate it to the big things in life. It also just makes you appear **witty** and **clever** to link unrelated elements together like metaphors usually do.

The metaphor doesn't really have to be good, or make much sense. It just has to sound interesting – people will draw their own conclusions if there is any sort of link.

Again, using the example where someone loses a pair of sunglasses after riding a rollercoaster, you can reply something like the following: "Rollercoasters are like charities, I donate so many things because I lose something every time I ride one!"

Or, "Losing things is like when you have a rock in your shoe, it's so annoying."

Or, "Sunglasses are my savior on most days, I would be lost without them."

This communicates to the person that you are a **deep thinker** and it also communicates to the person that what they said resonated with you enough for you to draw these connections.

Of course, in an improv comedy setting, the whole point is to get laughs.

In a personal conversation setting, when you throw out a very deep and heavy metaphor, it cannot help but get the listener to bond with you on a deep and **personal** level.

This person feels that you appreciate their ideas enough to create a metaphor that plays on their main message.

The drawback to the metaphor angle is just like the drawback to the philosophy angle. You cheapen it if you **overuse** it. You cheapen it when you make connections that are very shallow and cast a bad light on the experience your conversation partner had.

When you use HPM correctly, you will never run out of things to say, **ever**.

But you don't need to use it just as a last resort. HPM works because it is **universal** – everyone has beliefs and thoughts on daily occurrences, and everyone has stories about their daily lives that they enjoy sharing.

HPM is a **framework** for sharing relatable topics that become the low hanging fruit for conversations to begin and go deeper.

Try this exercise:

This is best done through text or instant messaging. Look over the transcript of one of your recent digital exchanges.

Write down a list of 5 topics or subtopics. You can even just write down a few statements that you replied to.

Now time to practice HPM. For each topic or statement, come up with 4 personal stories, 4 ways to demonstrate how you feel about it, and 3 metaphors that show a deeper understanding of the topic at hand.

This will be difficult at first, but deep connections aren't built by small talking about the weather. Deep connections are built with shared values, beliefs, and opinions – HPM cuts to the core and addresses all of those at once.

Conclusion

It should be abundantly clear at this point that improv comedy functions almost completely parallel to memorable conversations.

When you think about it, even on a shallow level, they have so much in common.

They have the same premise – an interaction that has the potential to be great and memorable, if the two parties can interact with each other to create enough flow.

They have the same path to greatness and memorability – rules and techniques to make sure that there is maximum flow, collaboration, and adaptability.

They even have the same end goal – an interaction that is greatly enjoyed by both parts with the potential to lead to deeper connections.

It simply makes too much sense to apply the improv comedy framework that years of intensive practice and practicum have produced to our conversation skills.

It's my hope and desire that you learn from the rules within, but go a step beyond and seek out your own ways to create conversational flow. The best rules are the rules that work for you, and everyone's mind works a slightly different way for a one-size-fits-all set of rules to be perfect for everyone.

In the meantime, upon discovering how difficult these principles are, another vote of respect for Will Ferrell.

Sincerely,

Patrick King
Dating and Social Skills Coach
www.PatrickKingConsulting.com

P.S. If you enjoyed this book, please don't be shy and drop me a line, leave a review, or both! I love reading feedback, and reviews are the lifeblood of Kindle books, so they are always welcome and greatly appreciated.

Other books by Patrick King include:

CHATTER: Small Talk, Charisma, and How to Talk to Anyone

MAGNETIC: How to Impress, Connect, and Influence

Conversationally Speaking: WHAT to Say, WHEN to Say It, and HOW to Never Run Out of Things To Say

Cheat Sheet

Rule 1.

In response to someone else's suggestion, thought, or topic, always say "Yes, AND..." to move to their topic and add something to it, to keep the conversation flowing.

Rule 2.

React to everything put in front of you, because it was probably put there for a reason.

Rule 3.

Don't force others to answer broad questions because it puts a conversational burden on them and interrupts banter.

Rule 4.

Be as present and observant as possible so you can see where an interaction is coming from, and where it wants to go.

Rule 5.

Provide specific details for people to relate to, react to, and run with.

Rule 6.

Never lead with "No." because it disregards the direction that someone wants to go and makes it more difficult to work towards a common, shared goal.

Rule 7.

Interactions must always be moving ahead, because staying stagnant is death.

Rule 8.

Improv is about creating entertaining and interesting situations for the other players and the audience.

Rule 9.

Great improv is a result of the creativity in spontaneous situations, and set agendas and outlines put a very low ceiling on that.

Rule 10.

Since you are all working towards a shared goal, you are everyone else's supporting actor so do your best to make your fellow improv players look good and they will do the same to you.

Rule 11.

Reincorporate specific elements from earlier in the interaction in different contexts for big laughs.

Rule 12.

There's a reason why the people involved in improv comedy are called players and why performances are treated like sports games – it's something that people practice for, to produce the best result like any sport.

Rule 13.

Improv comedy is about playing off others, and you can't do that if you are constantly waiting for your turn to talk and not listening to others. Sometimes you just need to shut up and listen patiently.

Rule 14.

If all else fails, talk about history, philosophy, or metaphor.